# CONTENTS

# AERIAL ACROBATS

# PLANT LOVERS

# WELCOME...

THIS FASCINATING ANNUAL IS PACKED FULL OF FEARSOME FACTS ABOUT THE DEADLIEST ANIMALS OUT THERE. WHICH ONES BITE? WHICH ARE POISONOUS? WHICH ARE MOST LIKELY TO KILL YOU? INSIDE YOU'LL DISCOVER WHICH ANIMAL THE DEADLIEST VENOM, WHICH ONE COULD SWALLOW YOU WHOLE AND WHICH CREATURE FEEDS ONLY ON BLOOD!

WE ALSO GO BACK IN TIME TO WHEN DINOSAURS ROAMED THE EARTH TO GIVE YOU THE LOWDOWN ON THESE PREHISTORIC BEASTS. PLUS, YOU CAN GIVE YOUR BRAIN A WORKOUT WITH SOME AWESOME ANIMAL PUZZLES.

LOOK OUT FOR THESE SYMBOLS THROUGHOUT THE ANNUAL. THEY RATE JUST HOW DEADLY EACH ANIMAL IS. THE MORE SKULL AND CROSSBONES THERE ARE, THE MORE DANGEROUS THE ANIMAL IS TO HUMANS!

# WELCOME TO THE DEADLY PREDATORS...

**AWESOME!**
GREAT WHITES CAN GLIDE THROUGH THE OCEAN AT SPEEDS OF UP TO 24 KM/H (15 MPH).

# GREAT WHITE SHARK
*(Carcharodon carcharias)*

**WOW!**
GREAT WHITES ARE ACTUALLY MOSTLY GREY. THEIR NAME COMES FROM THEIR WHITE UNDERBELLY.

RATED

Animal class: Fish

| | |
|---|---|
| Home: | Cool, coastal waters worldwide |
| Lifespan: | Around 70 years |
| Length: | Average of 4.6m (15ft) |
| Weight: | 2.5 tonnes (398st) or more |

**AMAZING!**
THE GREAT WHITE HAS THE STRONGEST BITE OF ANY LIVING SPECIES.

**Diet:**
Carnivorous great whites feast on a variety of sea creatures, including seals, small toothed whales, turtles and sea lions.

**Hunting style:**
These super sharks have an amazing sense of smell which they use to hunt down their prey. They swim underwater, surfacing at the last moment to snatch their victim in their deadly jaws.

**Killer teeth:**
Up to 300 triangular, serrated teeth are packed in rows inside the mouth of each great white.

**Deadly rating:**
High. More shark attacks are blamed on great whites than any other shark species. Their killer teeth and powerful jaws can cause serious injury and sometimes death.

**RECORD BREAKER**
THE MENACING GREAT WHITE HOLDS THE RECORD AS THE WORLD'S MOST DANGEROUS SHARK.

## FOOD CHAIN

Fish      Sea Lion      Great White Shark

# BLACK MAMBA
## (Dendroaspis polylepis)

**WOW!**

BLACK MAMBAS ARE ACTUALLY AN OLIVE-GREY COLOUR. THEY GET THEIR NAME FROM THE COLOUR OF THE INSIDE OF THEIR MOUTH, WHICH THEY SHOW WHEN FEELING THREATENED.

| | |
|---|---|
| Animal class: | Reptile |
| Home: | Eastern part of tropical Africa |
| Lifespan: | Up to 11 years |
| Length: | Up to 4.3m (14ft) |
| Weight: | Up to 1.6kg (3½lb) |

**Diet:**
Rodents, squirrels and other snakes are all on the menu for these hungry reptiles.

**Hunting style:**
Fearsome black mambas bite their prey once or twice then wait for their venom to paralyse and kill.

**Deadly rating:**
Extremely high. If bitten by a black mamba a human will die within 20 minutes without antivenom.

**RECORD BREAKER**
THE BLACK MAMBA IS THE WORLD'S FASTEST LAND SNAKE. IT'S BEEN RECORDED AT TOP SPEEDS OF 16-19 KM/H (10-12 MPH) IN SHORT BURSTS.

# PYTHON
## (Pythonidae)

**WOW!**

PYTHONS DON'T HAVE VERY GOOD EYESIGHT SO RELY ON THEIR OTHER SENSES TO FIND PREY.

**RECORD BREAKER**
THE OLDEST RELIABLE RECORDED AGE FOR A SNAKE IS 47 YEARS AND 6 MONTHS FOR A PYTHON AT PHILADELPHIA ZOO.

| | |
|---|---|
| Animal class: | Reptile |
| Home: | Asia, Africa and Australia |
| Lifespan: | Up to 40 years |
| Length: | Up to 7m (23ft) |
| Weight: | Up to 160kg (25st) |

**Diet:**
What a python eats depends on its size. Its diet may include birds, lizards, pigs and monkeys.

**Hunting style:**
Deadly pythons grab their prey with their long teeth then squeeze it to death before swallowing it whole.

**Deadly rating:**
Medium. As pythons are nonvenomous they aren't normally considered dangerous to humans but there are stories of African rock pythons swallowing people whole.

# Polar Bear

## *(Ursus maritimus)*

**RATED**

**WOW!**
POLAR BEARS CAN SWIM WITHOUT STOPPING FOR UP TO 10 DAYS.

**WOW!**
UNDERNEATH THEIR WHITE FUR POLAR BEARS HAVE BLACK SKIN TO ABSORB THE SUN'S RAYS.

**WOW!**
HAIRY POLAR BEARS EVEN HAVE FUR ON THE BOTTOM OF THEIR PAWS.

Animal class: Mammal

| | |
|---|---|
| Home: | Arctic |
| Lifespan: | 25-30 years |
| Length: | Up to 2.4m (8ft) |
| Weight: | 408kg-725kg (64st-114st) |

**Diet:**
Seals are polar bears' main source of food although they may also eat walruses, carrion, narwhals and beluga whales. In summer they'll even snack on grass and berries.

**Hunting style:**
Patient polar bears wait on sheets of ice for seals to pop up through breathing holes before pouncing on their prey. They will also target basking seals by creeping up on them and going in for the kill.

**Killer teeth:**
Polar bears have 42 teeth which are used to grasp and tear their food. Rather than chewing, polar bears usually swallow their meat in large chunks.

**Deadly rating:**
Medium. Polar bears will attack humans when they feel threatened by their presence. Polar bears are adapting to hunt on land and scavenge rubbish, when they are struggling to reach their usual food sources.

## FOOD CHAIN

Fish     Seal     Polar Bear

# PREDATOR PUZZLE

THE NAMES OF ANIMALS BELOW ARE HIDDEN IN THIS WORDSEARCH. CAN YOU SPOT EACH ONE?

 SHARK

 LION

 HYENA

 TIGER

 SNAKE

 SPIDER

 SCORPION

 WOLF

 BEAR

 WHALE

```
A Y V W S C U L S S V Q U C N
B I H O Q X M P Y U P D E A L
W H A L E K I R G D F Y G M F
A C X F F D S E G U Y B I Z E
A C G S E D C G E J J C U J C
H N M R B R O I D L L W T K J
T C E E E S R T F R Z Y T Q W
I S A Y Q I P S Q Y G Q V O E
X R C U H E I S A X A E F U O
S M M W K I O C P B L C X R O
H Y S A E L N S C C M J F V H
H Q N F O N C M X L G X L H Q
H S V Q Z G G U X Q I T M D G
M Z B M S L C C X C V O D J D
Q H R G M I Z K R A H S N G C
```

NAMES CAN GO DOWN, ACROSS, DIAGONALLY AND BACKWARDS.

ANSWERS ON PAGES 76-77 11

# WHICH ONE?

**WHICH OF THESE POWERFUL PREDATORS HAS THE STRONGEST BITE? USE THE CLUES BELOW TO WORK OUT THE ANSWER.**

## IT IS A CARNIVORE.

**KILLER WHALE**

**PYTHON**

## IT DOESN'T HAVE LEGS.

## IT LIVES IN THE SEA.

**GREAT WHITE SHARK**

**LION**

**KOMODO DRAGON**

## IT IS A FISH.

ANSWER:

# ICY MAZE

## AMAZING!

POLAR BEARS HAVE BEEN SEEN COVERING THEIR DARK NOSES WITH A PAW OR A PIECE OF SNOW WHEN STALKING SEALS ON THE OPEN ICE.

◀ START

THIS HUNGRY POLAR BEAR IS LOOKING FOR SOME LUNCH. GUIDE IT THROUGH THE MAZE TO THE UNSUSPECTING SEAL.

ANSWERS ON PAGES 76-77 13

RATED!

# KILLER WHALE
## (Orcinus orca)

**WOW!**
ALTHOUGH THEY ARE CALLED KILLER WHALES, ORCAS ARE ACTUALLY THE LARGEST DOLPHIN SPECIES.

**WOW!**
A MALE ORCA'S DORSAL FIN CAN GROW AS TALL AS SOME MEN, REACHING 1.8M (6FT).

Animal class: Mammal

| | |
|---|---|
| Home: | Arctic and Antarctic |
| Lifespan: | 50-90 years |
| Length: | Males up to 9.8m (32ft), females up to 8.5m (28ft) |
| Weight: | Males up to 9,000kg (1,417st), females up to 5,500kg (866st) |

**Diet:**
Hungry killer whales gobble up fish and marine mammals including penguins, sea lions, sharks, sea turtles and other whales. These brave beasts will even attack animals much larger than themselves.

**Hunting style:**
Deadly orcas hunt in pods of up to 40. They work together to herd fish into small areas to make them easy prey or to surround and attack bigger animals such as sperm whales. In the Antarctic, clever killer whales use their tails to make waves to wash seals off the ice into the water.

**Killer teeth:**
Orcas have around 45 teeth designed to rip and tear prey. They will even swallow smaller animals, such as sea lions, whole!

**WOW!**
NO OTHER ANIMALS HUNT KILLER WHALES. THEY ARE TOP OF THE FOOD CHAIN

**Deadly rating:**
Medium. In captivity there have been several fatal attacks on humans but there are only a few cases of wild killer whales attacking people and no fatal encounters.

## FOOD CHAIN

Fish     Sea Lion     Killer Whale

# HYENA
## (Hyaenidae)

Animal class: Mammal

| | |
|---|---|
| Home: | Africa |
| Lifespan: | Up to 25 years |
| Length: | 95cm-165cm |
| | (3ft-5½ft) |
| Weight: | 50kg-86kg (7¾st-13½st) |

Diet:
Hyenas are scavengers and happily dine on other animals' leftovers. When hunting for their own prey they'll target antelope, birds, lizards and snakes.

Hunting style:
Ferocious hyenas work in packs to take down their prey. They use their sharp teeth to bite, then drag their victim to the ground.

Deadly rating:
Medium. Although hyenas have been known to turn on humans these attacks are rare.

**AMAZING!**
A HYENA'S POWERFUL JAW IS CAPABLE OF CRUSHING BONES.

# BROWN BEAR
## (Ursus arctos)

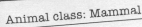

Animal class: Mammal

| | |
|---|---|
| Home: | North America, Europe and Asia |
| Lifespan: | Average of 25 years |
| Length: | Up to 177cm (5ft 8in) |
| Weight: | Up to 318kg (50st) |

Diet:
Ginormous brown bears have an appetite to match their size. Their diet includes nuts, berries, roots, leaves, fruit and small animals.

Hunting style:
Resourceful bears use their long claws to upturn logs, scrape bark and disturb earth mounds when looking for lunch.

Deadly rating:
Medium. Brown bears can be extremely dangerous to humans if they are surprised or if a person gets between a mother and her cubs.

**WOW!**
ADULT BROWN BEARS ARE AT THE TOP OF THE FOOD CHAIN.

# DEADLY SUMS

WHICH OF THESE VENOMOUS ANIMALS IS THE MOST POISONOUS? ADD UP THE NUMBERS FOR EACH ONE TO SEE WHICH HAS THE HIGHEST SCORE.

## BLACK MAMBA

| 13 | 8 | 11 | 25 | |

## POISON DART FROG

| 20 | 21 | 4 | 19 | |

## DEATHSTALKER SCORPION

| 16 | 5 | 12 | 19 | |

## BRAZILIAN HUNTSMAN SPIDER

| 18 | 9 | 22 | 10 | |

# GREY WOLF

*(Canis lupus)*

RATED

**Animal class: Mammal**

| | |
|---|---|
| Home: | Europe, America, Canada, Alaska, Asia |
| Lifespan: | 6-8 years |
| Length: | 91cm-160cm (2½-5ft) |
| Weight: | 18kg-79kg (2¾st-12½st) |

Diet:
Grey wolves mostly munch on large hooved animals such as deer, moose and mountain goats.

Hunting style:
Cunning wolves hunt in packs. They either ambush animals or chase their prey to tire it out before going in for the kill.

Deadly rating: Medium.
The grey wolf is the only wolf that is a potential threat to humans. It is more than capable of killing a person if it wanted to.

# SIBERIAN TIGER

*(Panthera tigris)*

RATED

**Animal class: Mammal**

| | |
|---|---|
| Home: | Russia, China, North Korea |
| Lifespan: | 10-15 years |
| Length: | Up to 3.3m (10½ft) |
| Weight: | Up to 300kg (47st) |

Diet:
These powerful hunters travel for miles to find food. They devour large animals such as deer and wild boar and snack on smaller prey such as rabbits.

Hunting style:
Stealthy tigers hunt at night. They lie in wait for potential prey before creeping closer and pouncing.

Deadly rating:
High. Tigers can kill humans although most attacks are the result of accidental close encounters or confrontations.

# AFRICAN LION
## (Panthera leo)

**RATED**

**AWESOME!**
AN ADULT MALE'S ROAR CAN BE HEARD UP TO 8KM (5 MILES) AWAY.

**WOW!**
FEMALE LIONS ARE THE MAIN HUNTERS IN A PRIDE.

Animal class: Mammal

| | |
|---|---|
| Home: | Africa |
| Lifespan: | 10-14 years |
| Length: | 1.4m-2m (4½ft-6½ft) |
| Weight: | 120kg-190kg (19st-30st) |

Diet:
Zebras, antelope and wildebeest are firm favourites for famished lions.

Hunting style:
Cooperative lions work together as a team to capture their prey. They hunt from dusk until dawn and stalk their victims before a short and powerful attack.

Mean teeth:
Fierce lions have 30 teeth. Their wide-opening mouths mean they are able to give really big bites.

Deadly rating:
High. Lions normally try to avoid people but attacks do happen, usually as a result of people getting too close.

**WOW!** LIONS ARE THE ONLY CATS THAT LIVE IN GROUPS.

## FOOD CHAIN

Grass     Zebra     African Lion

# POISON DART FROG

## (Dendrobatidae)

**Animal class: Amphibian**

Home:  Central and South America

Length: Up to 6cm (2½in)

Weight: Average of 28g (1oz)

Diet:
Meat-loving poison dart
frogs feast on insects and termites.

Hunting style:
Poison dart frogs shoot out
their long, sticky tongue to
catch unsuspecting prey.

Deadly rating:
Extremely high. These frogs secrete a
toxic poison from their skin. Several
species' secretions are so toxic that just
a tiny smear is enough to kill a human.

**WOW!**
POISON DART FROGS ARE BRIGHTLY COLOURED TO WARN OFF PREDATORS.

# KOMODO DRAGON

## (Varanus komodoensis)

**Animal class: Reptile**

Home:   Five Indonesian islands

Length: Average of 2.3m (7½ft)
        for males

Weight: Up to 150kg (23½st)

Diet:
Any animal it can catch including
carrion, pigs and water buffalo.

Hunting style:
Sneaky dragons lie in wait for passing
prey before knocking it over with their
huge feet then shredding it to death with
their sharp teeth.

Deadly rating:
High. On the island of Komodo, local
villagers and tourists have
fallen prey to the dragons.

**AWESOME!**
THE KOMODO DRAGON IS THE LARGEST LIZARD IN THE WORLD.

# DEATH STALKER SCORPION

## (Leiurus quinquestriatus)

**Animal class: Invertebrate**

Home:  Eastern Africa

Length: Up to 11.5cm (4½in)

Weight: Up to 2.5g (9/100oz)

Diet:
Insects, earthworms, spiders and centipedes
are all on the menu for these feared predators.

Hunting style:
Stealthy scorpions hunt at night, ambushing their
victims then crushing them with their pincers.

**WOW!**
THE DEATH STALKER IS THE MOST VENOMOUS SCORPION IN THE WORLD.

Deadly rating:
Medium. A sting from a
death stalker scorpion doesn't usually kill an
adult but it can cause respiratory problems,
excessive sweating and fluid on the lungs.

# BRAZILIAN HUNTSMAN SPIDER

## (Phoneutria fera)

**Animal class: Invertebrate**

Home:  South and Central America

Size:   Leg span of up to 15cm (6in)

Diet:
Brazilian huntsman
spiders dine on large insects,
small lizards and mice.

Hunting style:
These wandering spiders don't make webs to
catch their prey, instead they hunt freely on
the forest floor at night.

**WOW!**
THE BRAZILIAN HUNTSMAN IS THE WORLD'S MOST VENOMOUS SPIDER.

Deadly rating:
High. The huntsman spider is extremely
aggressive and will bite if provoked. Symptoms
include excruciating pain, hypothermia
and breathing difficulties. Thanks to an
effective antivenom deaths are now rare.

# WHICH WAY?

## THERE'S ONLY ONE CORRECT PATH THROUGH THIS MAZE – CAN YOU USE THE ANIMAL KEY TO FOLLOW IT?

**TURN RIGHT**

**TURN LEFT**

**MOVE DOWN**

**START**

**FINISH**

# WORD PLAY

USE THE LETTERS IN DEADLIEST TO MAKE AS MANY WORDS AS YOU CAN, SUCH AS DEAD, EATS AND STEAL. WRITE YOUR ANSWERS BELOW THEN CHECK OUT YOUR SCORE.

## "DEADLIEST"

Write your answers here

1.

2.

3.

4.

5.

6.

7.

8.

9.

10.

**WHAT'S YOUR SCORE?**
0-3 WORDS: GOOD GOING!
4-7 WORDS: RESULT!
8 OR MORE WORDS: WOW!

# INTRODUCING THE SEA DWELLERS...

# SALTWATER CROCODILE
## (Crocodylus porosus)

**RATED**

**Animal class: Reptile**

| | |
|---|---|
| Home: | Asia, Australia |
| Lifespan: | Average of 70 years |
| Length: | Average of 5.2m (17ft) |
| Weight: | Average of 454kg (71½st) |

**Diet:**
Salties aren't fussy and will eat anything they can get their jaws around, including water buffalo, wild boar and monkeys.

**AMAZING!**
CROCODILES CAN TACKLE PREY BIGGER THAN THEMSELVES.

**Hunting style:**
Sneaky crocodiles hide just below the water's surface and wait patiently for prey to come and drink. Then, quick as a flash, they'll emerge, grab their prey and hold it underwater until it drowns.

**Killer teeth:**
A crocodile's cone-shaped teeth are made even more deadly by the ferocious snap of their jaw.

**Deadly rating:**
Extremely high. Dangerous salties have exceptionally strong bites and kill around 2,000 people every year.

**AWESOME!**
SALTIES CAN STAY UNDERWATER FOR MORE THAN AN HOUR.

## FOOD CHAIN

Frog          Wild Boar          Saltwater Crocodile

# TIGER SHARK

*(Galeocerdo cuvier)*

**WOW!**
CAR NUMBER PLATES, LEATHER COATS AND PAINT CANS HAVE ALL BEEN FOUND IN THE STOMACHS OF TIGER SHARKS.

Animal class: Fish

| | |
|---|---|
| Home: | Tropical waters worldwide |
| Lifespan: | Average of 15 or more years |
| Length: | 3m-4.3m (10ft-14ft) |
| Weight: | 385kg-635kg (60½st-100st) |

Diet:
Tiger sharks have been given the nickname 'garbage-can sharks' because they'll eat anything they find in the water, including other sharks, seabirds and crabs.

Hunting style:
Greedy tiger sharks use their saw-like teeth to slice through flesh, sinew and bone.

Deadly rating:
High. Tiger sharks are second only to great whites for attacking people. They're not likely to swim away after biting a human.

# BLUEFISH

*(Pomatomus saltatrix)*

**AMAZING!**
BLUEFISH ARE SOMETIMES NICKNAMED 'MARINE PIRANHAS' BECAUSE OF THEIR RAZOR SHARP TEETH.

Animal class: Fish

| | |
|---|---|
| Home: | Atlantic, Indian and South Pacific Oceans |
| Lifespan: | Up to 9 years |
| Length: | Up to 1.2m (4ft) |
| Weight: | 7.9kg (1¼st) |

Diet:
Greedy bluefish mainly gorge on menhaden and mullet. They are also known to regurgitate so they can eat again.

Hunting style:
Bluefish feast in a feeding frenzy. They swim in packs and kill more prey than they eat, leaving a trail of carnage behind them.

Deadly rating:
Low. Aggressive bluefish have strong conical teeth and have been known to bite humans. Although it wouldn't kill you, it would certainly hurt!

# BOX JELLYFISH
## (Chironex fleckeri)

**RATED**

**WOW!**
A BIG BOX JELLYFISH HAS ENOUGH VENOM TO KILL 60 PEOPLE.

**WOW!**
IN AUSTRALIA, MORE PEOPLE ARE KILLED BY BOX JELLYFISH THAN BY SHARKS AND CROCODILES COMBINED.

Animal class: Invertebrate

**RECORD BREAKER**
BOX JELLYFISH ARE PROBABLY THE MOST VENOMOUS ANIMAL IN THE WORLD.

| | |
|---|---|
| Home: | Australia, Asia |
| Lifespan: | Up to one year |
| Length: | Tentacles up to 4.6m (15ft) |
| Weight: | Up to 2kg (4¼lbs) |

**Diet:**
Meat-loving box jellyfish dine on other sea creatures including shrimp, fish and prawns.

**Hunting style:**
Box jellyfish move through the water using their 24 eyes to search for prey. Victims are immediately stunned or killed by their potent venom.

**Killer sting:**
The feared box jellyfish has up to 60 long tentacles which are covered with millions of stinging capsules. Venom is delivered from the capsules into the skin of any creature that touches a tentacle. Other capsules discharge a sticky substance which make the tentacles stick to the victim. Ouch!

**Deadly rating:**
Extremely high. In the last decade at least 70 people have been killed in Australia by a box jellyfish sting, some have died within 4 minutes.

**WOW!**
BIZARRELY, BOX JELLYFISH STINGS CAN'T GET THROUGH WOMEN'S TIGHTS!

## FOOD CHAIN

 Shrimp

 Sea turtle

 Box Jellyfish

24

# SHARK SIZES

CAN YOU PUT THESE SNAPPY SHARKS IN ORDER OF SIZE? START WITH THE SMALLEST AND WRITE YOUR ANSWERS BELOW

SMALLEST

LARGEST

ANSWERS ON PAGES 76-77 25

# RECORD BREAKER

THE BEAUTIFUL BOX JELLYFISH HOLDS A DEADLY WORLD RECORD. CROSS OUT ALL THE WORDS BELOW THAT APPEAR TWICE. THE REMAINING WORDS WILL REVEAL THE RECORD.

SWIM

FISH        MOST        WATER

SEA    VENOMOUS    FIN    WATER

ANIMAL    FISH    IN    SWIM

THE    SEA    WORLD    FIN

**WOW!**
IT TAKES APPROXIMATELY 3M (10FT) OF BOX JELLYFISH TENTACLE TO ADMINISTER A FATAL DOSE OF POISON TO A PERSON.

## THE BOX JELLYFISH IS THE...

# CREATURE COUNT

THESE FEROCIOUS FISH HAVE GOT THEMSELVES ALL JUMBLED UP! HOW MANY OF EACH ONE CAN YOU COUNT? WRITE YOUR ANSWERS IN THE CIRCLES.

BLUEFISH ◯  NEEDLEFISH ◯  BARRACUDA ◯

# STINGRAY
## (Myliobatoidei)

RATED

**WOW!**
RAYS SPEND MOST OF THEIR TIME PARTIALLY BURIED IN SAND ON THE OCEAN FLOOR.

**WOW!**
A RAY'S MOUTH IS ON ITS UNDERBELLY.

**AWESOME!**
A STINGRAY'S COLOUR CAMOUFLAGES IT FROM PREDATORS.

Animal class: Fish

| | |
|---|---|
| Home: | Temperate seas worldwide |
| Lifespan: | 15-25 years |
| Length: | Up to 2m (6½ft) |
| Weight: | Up to 358kg (56st) |

Diet:
Stingrays like to eat small sea creatures such as shrimp, squid, clams, oysters and mussels.

Hunting style:
Laid-back rays have an electrical sensor in their mouth which allows them to detect the natural electric rays of nearby prey. Many species have teeth for crushing shellfish.

Killer sting:
Stingrays have a venomous barb located on their tail which they use to protect themselves. A frightened ray will flip its tail up and strike whatever is in front of it.

Deadly rating:
Medium. Passive stingrays rarely attack humans but when they do it is extremely painful and can be deadly if their barb pierces the heart or abdominal area. Most attacks result from people accidentally stepping on rays.

## FOOD CHAIN

 →  →

Mussels          Stingray          Hammerhead Shark

# MORAY EEL

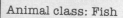

*(Muraenidae)*

**AWESOME!**
IN SOME COUNTRIES PEOPLE EAT MORAY EELS BUT THEIR FLESH CAN BE TOXIC AND CAUSE ILLNESS OR DEATH.

Animal class: Fish

Home: Warm waters worldwide
Length: Up to 1.5m (5ft)
Weight: Average of 13.6kg (2¼st)
Diet:
Moray eels dine on smaller fish, octopuses, squid, cuttlefish and crustaceans.

Hunting style:
Moray eels have two sets of teeth. They grab their victim with the first set, then the second set, located in the throat, lunges forward drawing the prey in.

Deadly rating:
Medium. Morays will only attack humans if disturbed but they can be quite vicious and those chainsaw teeth will give a nasty nip.

# NEEDLEFISH

*(Belonidae)*

**WOW!**
DANGEROUS NEEDLEFISH CAN THROW THEMSELVES OUT OF THE WATER TO BECOME FLYING DAGGERS.

Animal class: Fish

Home: Tropical and subtropical waters
Length: 3cm-95cm (1¼in-37½in)
Weight: Up to 4.8kg (10½lb)
Diet:
Smaller fish are needlefishes' meal of choice.

Hunting style:
Needlefish have long, narrow jaws crammed full of sharp teeth. They catch their prey by sweeping their heads upwards.

Deadly rating:
Medium. Attacks are rare but people have been seriously hurt when stabbed by the needlefish's sharp jaws.

# RED LION FISH

*(Pterois volitans)*

**WOW!**
WITH THEIR RED AND WHITE STIRPES AND IMPRESSIVE FINS, RED LION FISH ARE POPULAR AQUARIUM FISH.

Animal class: Fish

Home: Warm oceans worldwide
Length: 30cm-38cm (12in-15in)
Weight: Up to 1.2kg (2½lb)
Diet:
Lionfish certainly aren't fussy eaters – they'll consume over 70 species of other fish.

Hunting style:
Stealthy lion fish lie in wait then corner their prey with their large fins before gulping it down whole.

Deadly rating:
Medium. Lion fish have venomous spines on their fins which can deliver painful puncture wounds. The venom can cause nausea and breathing difficulties.

# BARRACUDA

*(Sphyraena)*

**AMAZING!**
BARRACUDAS HAVE BEEN AROUND FOR 50 MILLION YEARS.

Animal class: Fish

Home: Tropical and subtropical oceans worldwide
Length: Up to 165cm (5½ft)
Weight: Up to 24kg (3¾st)
Diet:
Snapper, tuna, mullet and herring are all on the menu for hungry barracudas.

Hunting style:
Speedy barracudas race through the water to catch unsuspecting prey before shredding it to pieces with their super sharp teeth.

Deadly rating:
Low. With their prominent, pointy teeth, barracudas look pretty scary but thankfully attacks on humans are rare.

# OCEAN PUZZLE

CAN YOU FIT THE NAMES OF THESE SEA DWELLERS INTO THE CROSSWORD BELOW? TWO LETTERS HAVE BEEN ADDED TO GET YOU STARTED.

CROCODILE     SHARK

OCTOPUS     RAY

EEL     BARRACUDA

JELLYFISH

ANSWERS ON PAGES 76-77

# PUFFERFISH
## (Tetraodontidae)

**Animal class: Fish**

| | |
|---|---|
| Home: | Warm and temperate waters worldwide |
| Lifespan: | Average of 10 years |
| Length: | Up to 91cm (3ft) |
| Weight: | 9kg-13.6kg (20lb-30lb) |

Diet:

Pufferfish consume invertebrates, algae and shellfish, such as clams and mussels.

Hunting style:

Pufferfish sneak up on their prey, then attack. With teeth that are fused together like a beak they are able to crack open shellfish with ease.

Deadly rating:

Extremely high. Poisonous pufferfish are eaten as a delicacy but must be prepared by specially trained chefs who remove the toxin, as even a tiny amount can cause death in as little as 20 minutes.

**WOW!**
IN JAPAN AROUND 30 PEOPLE DIE EACH YEAR AFTER EATING PUFFERFISH FLESH THAT HASN'T BEEN PROPERLY PREPARED.

# SURGEONFISH
## (Acanthuridae)

**AMAZING!**
THERE ARE OVER 75 DIFFERENT SPECIES OF SURGEONFISH.

**Animal class: Fish**

| | |
|---|---|
| Home: | Shallow water in the Indo-Pacific |
| Lifespan: | 12-15 years |
| Length: | Up to 26cm (10in) |
| Weight: | Average of 0.6kg (1½lb) |

Diet:

Surgeonfish are mostly herbivores but some species will eat meat.

Hunting style:

When surgeonfish aren't nibbling on algae or seaweed they scour the seabed for scraps left by other fish.

Deadly rating:

Low. Surgeonfish aren't usually a threat to humans but the razor sharp spines on each side of their body can give a painful slash.

# BLUE-RINGED OCTOPUS
## (Hapalochlaena)

RATED

**AMAZING!**
EACH BLUE-RINGED HAS ENOUGH VENOM TO PARALYSE 10 PEOPLE.

**AWESOME!**
IF PROVOKED, A BLUE-RINGED OCTOPUS' RINGS WILL FLASH BRIGHT BLUE AS A WARNING.

Animal class: Invertebrate

| | |
|---|---|
| Home: | Australia, Indonesia and the Philippines |
| Lifespan: | Two years |
| Length: | 12cm-20cm (5in-8in) |
| Weight: | Up to 28g (1oz) |

Diet:
This colourful little octopus mostly eats small crabs and shrimp.

**WOW!**
THE BLUE-RINGED IS THE ONLY OCTOPUS WHOSE VENOM IS DANGEROUS TO HUMANS.

Hunting style:
The venomous blue-ringed has sharp vision and hunts at night. It will pounce on its prey, grabbing it in its tentacles. Its bite releases a venom which paralyses then kills the victim.

Killer bite:
These pretty creatures have a parrot-like beak located above their eight arms. Their bite is relatively painless to humans and some victims don't even realise they've been attacked until the wound swells and the person feels a tingling around their mouth.

Deadly rating:
Medium. A bite from a blue-ringed octopus can kill in minutes. but they normally only attack if taken out of the water and provoked. If bitten, a person may have difficulty breathing and be unable to move but bizarrely some people are only mildly affected by the blue-ringed venom.

## FOOD CHAIN

Crab

Blue-ringed Octopus

Eel

# STONEFISH
## (Synanceiidae)

**AMAZING!**
THE SPINES OF THE INDIAN STONEFISH ARE SO SHARP THEY CAN PIERCE THE SOLE OF A BEACH SHOE.

**Animal class: Fish**

| Home: | Indo-Pacific, Australia, China, India |
| --- | --- |
| Lifespan: | 5-10 years |
| Length: | 35cm-51cm (14in-20in) |
| Weight: | Up to 2kg (4½lb) |

**Diet:**
Meat-eating stonefish feast on fish and shrimps.

**Hunting style:**
Stonefish rely on the element of surprise. Blending in to the environment, they wait patiently for prey to appear before quickly swallowing it.

**Deadly rating:**
Extremely high. Stonefish are so well camouflaged they're almost impossible to see. If a person treads on one, its spikes can give a painful, often fatal, wound.

# CONE SNAIL
## (Conus)

**WOW!**
A CONE SNAIL'S VENOM IS DELIVERED THROUGH ITS HOLLOW TEETH.

**Animal class: Invertebrate**

| Home: | Warm and tropical oceans worldwide |
| --- | --- |
| Lifespan: | 3-5 years |
| Length: | 1cm-20cm (½in-8in) |

**Diet:**
Small fish, marine worms and molluscs are all on the menu for colourful cone snails.

**Hunting style:**
Slow-moving cone snails use their powerful venom to paralyse their prey before consuming it.

**Deadly rating:**
Extremely high. Several species of cone snail are capable of killing humans with their venom. Non-fatal symptoms include impaired vision, dizziness and nausea.

# SEA CREATURE QUIZ

TICK THE BOXES TO ANSWER THESE UNDERWATER QUESTIONS.
IF YOU NEED HELP ALL THE ANSWERS CAN BE FOUND IN THE
'SEA DWELLERS' SECTION OF THIS ANNUAL.

1.  WHICH DANGEROUS ANIMAL KILLS UP TO 2,000 PEOPLE A YEAR?

SALTWATER CROCODILE ☐

NEEDLEFISH ☐

2.  WHICH FISH HAS POISONOUS SPINES ON ITS FINS?

RED LION FISH ☐

PUFFERFISH ☐

3.  WHICH ITEM HAS BEEN FOUND IN THE STOMACH OF A TIGER SHARK?

TRAFFIC CONE ☐

NUMBER PLATE ☐

4.  WHICH FISH IS NICKNAMED 'MARINE PIRANHA'?

BLUEFISH ☐

SURGEONFISH ☐

5.   WHICH SEA CREATURE HAS 24 EYES?

BOX JELLYFISH

BLUE-RINGED OCTOPUS

6.   WHICH FISH HAS A DEADLY BARB ON THE END OF ITS TAIL?

MORAY EEL

STINGRAY

7.   WHICH CREATURE IS EASILY CAMOUFLAGED UNDER THE SEA?

STONEFISH

CONE SNAIL

8.   WHICH FISH WILL EAT ANYTHING IT FINDS IN THE WATER?

TIGER SHARK

PUFFERFISH

9.   WHICH SEA CREATURE IS PROBABLY THE MOST VENOMOUS ANIMAL IN THE WORLD?

BARRACUDA

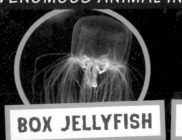

BOX JELLYFISH

ANSWERS ON PAGES 76-77

# WELCOME TO THE WORLD OF DINOSAURS...

## TYRANNOSAURUS

**AMAZING!**
THE TYRANNOSAURUS SKULL IS OVER 1.5M (5FT) LONG.

**WOW!**
THE *T-REX* WAS A SLOW RUNNER FOR ITS SIZE.

Meaning of name: Tyrant lizard

| | |
|---|---|
| Time period: | Late Cretaceous (67-65 million years ago) |
| Home: | Canada, USA |
| Length: | 12m (39ft) |
| Weight: | 7,000kg (1102st) |

Diet: Carnivore

Teeth:
The mighty *T-rex* had 60 sharp pointed teeth that were capable of crushing bone. Each one was up to 20cm (8in) long. With a bite around three times as strong as a lion's, these teeth were deadly.

Hunting style:
This fearsome beast had a sharp sense of smell which it would have used to track down prey and find dead bodies to scavenge.

RATED

**AWESOME!**
THE TYRANNOSAURUS WAS ONE OF THE MOST SUCCESSFUL CRETACEOUS PREDATORS.

# MAPUSAURUS

**AMAZING!**
MAPUSAURUS MAY HAVE BEEN THE LARGEST MEAT-EATING DINOSAUR.

Meaning of name: Earth lizard

| | |
|---|---|
| Time period: | Late Cretaceous (99-94 million years ago) |
| Home: | Argentina |
| Length: | 13m (43½ft) |
| Weight: | 3,000kg (472st) |

Diet: Carnivore

Description:
This ginormous beast walked on two legs and may have hunted in packs.

# DILOPHOSAURUS

**AWESOME!**
DILOPHOSAURUS HAD A KINK IN ITS UPPER JAW SIMILAR TO THAT OF MODERN DAY CROCODILES.

Meaning of name: Two-ridged lizard

| | |
|---|---|
| Time period: | Early Jurassic (190 million years ago) |
| Home: | USA |
| Length: | 6m (19½ft) |
| Weight: | 300kg (47st) |

Diet: Carnivore

Description:
This fast moving dinosaur had a mouth full of sharp and curved teeth and two bony crests on its head.

# STEGOSAURUS

RATED

**WOW!**

ALLOSAURUS AND CERATOSAURUS WERE AMONG THE DINOSAURS THAT PREYED ON STEGOSAURUS.

**AMAZING!**

IN MOST FOSSIL FINDS THE STEGOSAURUS BACK PLATES ARE SEPARATED FROM THE BODY.

Meaning of name: Roof lizard

| | |
|---|---|
| Time period: | Late Jurassic |
| | (156-144 million years ago) |
| Home: | USA |
| Length: | 9m (29½ft) |
| Weight: | 3,100kg (488st) |

Diet: Herbivore

Description:
This mighty plant eater had large bony plates along its back which were embedded into the skin.

Defending style:
The slow moving stegosaurus would have used its powerful spiked tail to defend itself against predators.

**AWESOME!**

STEGOSAURUS BACK PLATES MAY HAVE WARNED OFF ATTACKERS OR BEEN USED TO REGULATE TEMPERATURE.

# DINO DIFFERENCES

STUDY THESE DINOSAUR IMAGES CAREFULLY TO SPOT THE ODD ONE OUT IN EACH GROUP.

**1**

A  B  C

**2**

A  B  C

**3**

A  B  C

# SHADOW MATCH

CAN YOU WORK OUT WHICH DINOSAUR EACH OF THESE SHADOWS BELONGS TO? USE THE CLUES BELOW TO HELP YOU.

**AMAZING!**
MANY TYRANNOSAURUS FOSSILS REVEAL BITE MARKS FROM OTHER TYRANNOSAURS, SHOWING THAT THESE MIGHTY DINOSAURS USED TO FIGHT EACH OTHER.

A

B

C

D

**DIPLODOCUS**
CLUE: HAS A LONG NECK.

**TRICERATOPS**
CLUE: HAS THREE HORNS.

**STEGOSAURUS**
CLUE: HAS PLATES ON ITS BACK.

**TYRANNOSAURUS**
CLUE: WALKS ON TWO LEGS.

# T-REX TEASER

CRACK THE COLOUR CODE TO DISCOVER A FEARSOME
FACT ABOUT THE MIGHTY TYRANNOSAURUS.

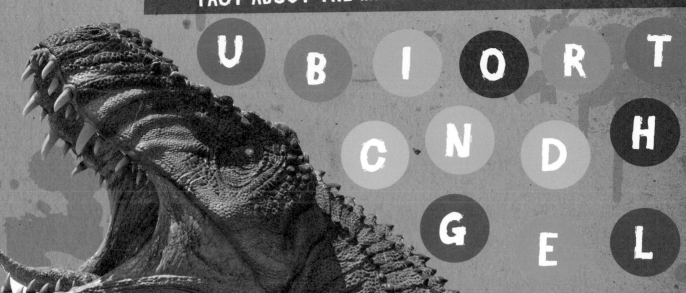

U  B  I  O  R  T

C  N  D  H

G  E  L

# VELOCIRAPTOR

RATED

Meaning of name: Quick plunderer

| | |
|---|---|
| Time period: | Late Cretaceous (84-80 million years ago) |
| Home: | Mongolia |
| Length: | 1.8m (6ft) |
| Weight: | 7kg (1st) |
| Diet: | Carnivore |

Teeth:
The velociraptor had lots of sharp pointy teeth to devour its prey.

Hunting style:
This deadly predator used its long tail for balance as it pounced on its prey before slashing its victims with sharp claws.

**AWESOME!**
LARGE EYES HELPED THE VELOCIRAPTOR SEEK OUT ITS PREY.

**WOW!**
THE VELOCIRAPTOR HAD A FINE, FEATHER-LIKE COVERING.

**AMAZING!**
A VELOCIRAPTOR'S CLAWS WERE 7CM (2¾IN) LONG.

# CARCHARODONTOSAURUS

Meaning of name: Carcharodon lizard

| | |
|---|---|
| Time period: | Late Cretaceous (98-94 million years ago) |
| Home: | North Africa |
| Length: | 15m (49ft) |
| Weight: | 8,000kg (1260st) |
| Diet: | Carnivore |

Description:
This meat-eating monster walked on two legs and had a long tail.

# UTAHRAPTOR

Meaning of name: Utah plunderer

| | |
|---|---|
| Time period: | Early Cretaceous (112-100 million years ago) |
| Home: | USA |
| Length: | 6m (20ft) |
| Weight: | 1,000kg (157st) |
| Diet: | Carnivore |

Description:
The utahraptor was a small theropod with lots of sharp, pointed teeth.

# ALLOSAURUS

Meaning of name: Other lizard

| | |
|---|---|
| Time period: | Late Jurassic (156-114 million years ago) |
| Home: | Portugal, USA |
| Length: | 12m (39ft) |
| Weight: | 2,000kg (315st) |
| Diet: | Carnivore |

Description: The allosaurus had long teeth that curved backwards to stop prey from escaping.

# ANKYLOSAURUS

Meaning of name: Stiff lizard

| | |
|---|---|
| Time period: | Late Cretaceous (74-67 million years ago) |
| Home: | Canada, USA |
| Length: | 7m (23ft) |
| Weight: | 4,000kg (630st) |
| Diet: | Herbivore |

Description:
This heavily armoured dinosaur had a wide skull and large club tail.

# NEXT IN LINE

## CAN YOU COMPLETE THESE SEQUENCES BY WORKING OUT WHICH DINOSAUR IS MISSING FROM EACH ONE?

**1**

SPINOSAURUS

GIGANOTOSAURUS

SPINOSAURUS

GIGANOTOSAURUS

GIGANOTOSAURUS

**2**

DIPLODOCUS

DIPLODOCUS

ANKYLOSAURUS

ANKYLOSAURUS

ANKYLOSAURUS

**3**

TYRANOSAURUS

TRICERATOPS

STEGOSAURUS

TYRANOSAURUS

TRICERATOPS

**4**

VELOCIRAPTOR

ALLOSAURUS

VELOCIRAPTOR

ALLOSAURUS

COELOPHYSIS

# TRICERATOPS

**RATED X**

**WOW!**

TRICERATOPS REMAINS HAVE SUGGESTED THAT THEY SPENT A LOT OF THEIR LIVES ALONE.

Meaning of name: Three-horned face

| | |
|---|---|
| Time period: | Late Cretaceous (67-66 million years ago) |
| Home: | USA |
| Length: | 9m (30ft) |
| Weight: | 5,500kg (866st) |
| Diet: | Herbivore |

Description:
With its menacing horns and 1.8m (5¾ft) wide neck frill, the triceratops would have certainly stood out from the crowd. Ferocious males used their horns to fight each other and to fend off attacking dinosaurs, while their huge frill acted as a shield.

# DIPLODOCUS

Meaning of name: Double beam

| | |
|---|---|
| Time period: | Late Jurassic (156-145 million years ago) |
| Home: | USA |
| Length: | 26m (84ft) |
| Weight: | 20,000kg (3,150st) |
| Diet: | Herbivore |

Description:
This long-tailed dinosaur moved on four legs and was able to reach high and low vegetation thanks to its long neck. Scientists believe that the diplodocus was able to hold its neck horizontally without using any muscles because of ligaments running from the hip to the neck.

**AMAZING!**

DIPLODOCUS HAD ROWS OF TEETH LIKE A COMB.

**RATED X**

RATED

# SPINOSAURUS

**AMAZING!**
THE SPINOSAURUS HAD A HUGE SAIL RUNNING ALONG THE LENGTH OF ITS BODY.

Meaning of name: Thorn lizard

| | |
|---|---|
| Time period: | Late Cretaceous (95-70 million years ago) |
| Home: | Egypt, Morocco |
| Length: | 18m (59ft) |
| Weight: | 4,000kg (630st) |
| Diet: | Carnivore |

Teeth:
Spinosaurus had flat, blade-like teeth with which to munch its prey.

Hunting style:
The spinosaurus used its long pointed snout to catch fish, much like a crocodile does today.

**AWESOME!**
SPINOSAURUS LIVED IN SWAMPY WATERS AS WELL AS ON DRY LAND.

**WOW!**
SPINOSAURUS WAS THE LONGEST MEAT-EATING DINOSAUR.

# GIGANOTOSAURUS

Meaning of name: Giant southern lizard

| | |
|---|---|
| Time period: | Early Cretaceous (112-90 million years ago) |
| Home: | Argentina |
| Length: | 12.5m (41ft) |
| Weight: | 8,000kg (1260st) |
| Diet: | Carnivore |

Description: This hunting machine had long, serrated teeth to slice through its prey.

# SAUROPHAGANAX

Meaning of name: King of the lizard eaters

| | |
|---|---|
| Time period: | Late Jurassic (154-142 million years ago) |
| Home: | USA |
| Length: | 12m (40ft) |
| Weight: | 3,000kg (472st) |
| Diet: | Carnivore |

Description: The saurophaganax walked on two legs and had a long, powerful tail.

# COELOPHYSIS

Meaning of name: Hollow form

| | |
|---|---|
| Time period: | Late Triassic (225-220 million years ago) |
| Home: | USA |
| Length: | 3m (10ft) |
| Weight: | 27kg (4st) |
| Diet: | Carnivore |

Description: This fast moving dinosaur had sharp teeth and grasping claws – perfect for holding onto its prey.

# MAJUNGASAURUS

Meaning of name: Majunga lizard

| | |
|---|---|
| Time period: | Late Cretaceous (84-71 million years ago) |
| Home: | Madagascar |
| Length: | 6m (20ft) |
| Weight: | 1,100kg (173st) |
| Diet: | Carnivore |

Description: Majungasaurus walked on two legs. It had large feet and small arms.

# UP CLOSE

CAN YOU WORK OUT WHICH CLOSE-UP BELONGS TO WHICH DINOSAUR? WRITE YOUR ANSWERS IN THE BOXES.

**A** UTAHRAPTOR

**B** MAJUNGASAURUS

**C** SAUROPHAGANAX

**D** MAPUSAURUS

**E** CARCHARODONTOSAURUS

1

2

3

4

5

# MIGHTY BITE

HOW MANY DEADLY TEETH DID A TYRANNOSAURUS HAVE? TO FIND OUT, WORK OUT WHICH LETTER IS MISSING FROM EACH CIRCLE BELOW THEN REARRANGE THE MISSING LETTERS TO SPELL A NUMBER.

A B C D
E F G H I J
K L M N O P
Q R S T U V
W Y Z

A B C D
E F G H I J
K L M N O P
Q R S U V W
X Y Z

A B C D
E F G H J
K L M N O P
Q R S T U V
W X Y Z

A B C D
E F G H I J
K L M N O P
Q R S T U V
W X Z

A B C D
E F G H I J
K L M N O P
Q R T U V W
X Y Z

# INTRODUCING THE AERIAL ACROBATS...

# VAMPIRE BAT
## (Desmodontidae)

RATED X

**AWESOME!**
TWO MINUTES INTO A FEED, VAMPIRE BATS BEGIN TO URINATE TO GET RID OF THE BLOOD PLASMA WHICH ISN'T NUTRITIOUS.

**WOW!**
IT TAKES ABOUT 20 MINUTES FOR A BAT TO DRINK THE BLOOD IT NEEDS, WHICH IS ABOUT TWO TABLESPOONS.

Animal class: Mammal

| | |
|---|---|
| Home: | Central and South America |
| Lifespan: | Average of 9 years |
| Length: | 6.5cm-6.9cm (2½in-2¾in) |
| Weight: | 40g (1½oz) |

**Diet:**
Bloodthirsty vampire bats feast on the blood of other animals, including birds, mules and horses.

**Hunting style:**
Under the cover of darkness, stealthy vampire bats choose their sleeping victim. Victims are usually unaware of the attack because the bat's bite is normally painless so they rarely wake up.

**Bloodsucking bite:**
Well-equipped bats have a heat sensor on their nose which they use to locate where blood flows close to the skin. They don't use their fangs to suck up the blood, instead they bite away a flap of skin and lick up the blood that flows from the wound.

**Deadly rating:**
Low. Bites to humans are very rare but have been known to happen. The main risk to people after a bat bite is being infected by rabies, a disease carried by a few vampire bats which can be fatal.

## FOOD CHAIN

Horse blood                    Vampire bat                    Owl

# MOSQUITO
## (Culicidae)

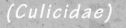

Animal class: Invertebrate

| | |
|---|---|
| Home: | Worldwide |
| Lifespan: | 2 weeks to 6 months |
| Length: | 3mm-19mm ($\frac{1}{8}$in-$\frac{3}{4}$in) |
| Weight: | 2.5mg (0.00009oz) |

Diet:

Pesky mosquitos eat flower and plant nectar. The females drink blood which they suck out of people and animals.

Hunting style:

These sneaky critters often bite without their victim being aware as their saliva numbs the wound. A tube-like proboscis inside the female's mouth pierces the skin and sucks up the blood.

Deadly rating:

Extremely high. This tiny insect is responsible for hundreds of thousands of human deaths each year, as a particular type of mosquito can carry the parasite which causes malaria.

**AMAZING!**
MOSQUITOS CAN DRINK UP TO THREE TIMES THEIR WEIGHT IN BLOOD.

# RED-TAILED HAWK
## (Buteo jamaicensis)

**WOW!**
RED-TAILED HAWKS CAN SPOT A MOUSE FROM 30M (100FT) UP IN THE AIR.

Animal class: Bird

| | |
|---|---|
| Home: | North America, Central America, West Indies |
| Lifespan: | Average of 21 years |
| Length: | 46cm-66cm (18in-26in) |
| Weight: | 0.7kg-1.4kg (1½lb-3lb) |

Diet:

Hungry hawks gobble up mice, squirrels, rabbits and reptiles.

Hunting style:

These expert hunters have awesome eyesight. They perch up high to look for prey then swoop down to catch it in their magnificent claws.

Deadly rating:

Low. In built-up areas hawks sometimes see humans as a threat and may swoop and attack with their talons to protect their territory. Luckily such attacks are rare.

RATED

# KILLER BEE
## (Africanised honey bee)

**AMAZING!**
IT WOULD TAKE AROUND 1,000 BEE STINGS TO DELIVER A FATAL DOSE OF VENOM TO AN ADULT.

**WOW!**
KILLER BEES HAVE ATTACKED PEOPLE MORE THAN 1KM (0.6 MILES) AWAY FROM THEIR NESTS.

Animal class: Invertebrate

**AWESOME!**
THE KILLER BEE IS A CROSS BETWEEN THE AFRICAN HONEY BEE AND THE EUROPEAN HONEY BEE.

| | |
|---|---|
| Home: | South, Central and North America |
| Lifespan: | 5 weeks to 3 years |
| Length: | Average of 1.3cm (½in) |

**Diet:**
Buzzing killer bees pollinate a wide variety of flowering plants.

**Hunting style:**
Killer bees forage for pollen early in the morning or late in the evening as the sun is setting.

**Killer defence:**
Ferocious killer bees fiercely defend their nests. Their venomous sting isn't actually any more potent than that of many other bees but, if threatened, they attack relentlessly in greater numbers which is what makes them deadlier.

**Deadly rating:**
High. Killer bees have been known to chase and attack people who approach their nests. Aggressive swarms have been blamed for nearly 1,000 deaths in the Amazon rainforest.

## FOOD CHAIN

Flower     Killer Bee     Bear

# PICTURE PUZZLE

CAN YOU PIECE THIS SNOWY OWL PICTURE BACK TOGETHER? DRAW LINES TO MATCH EACH SQUARE TO WHERE IT SHOULD GO ON THE GRID.

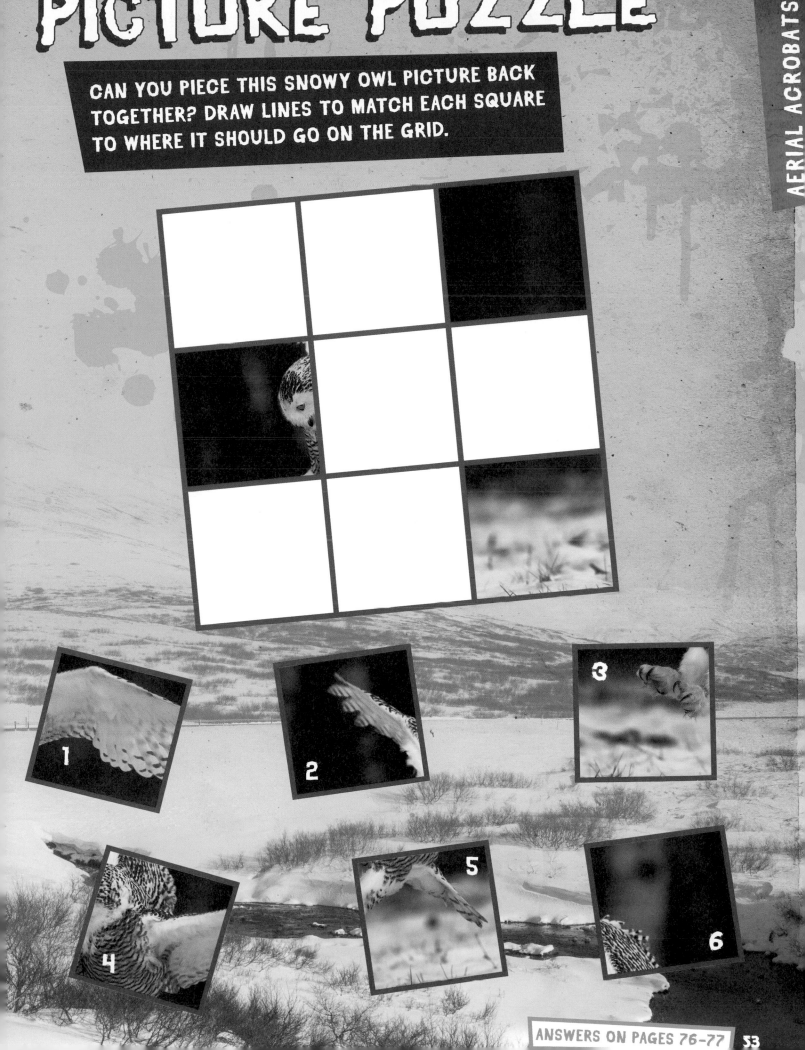

1

2

3

4

5

6

# HEADING HOME

THIS KILLER BEE HAS BECOME SEPARATED FROM ITS COLONY. CAN YOU GUIDE IT THROUGH THE MAZE BACK TO ITS HIVE?

ANSWERS ON PAGES 76-77

# FEARSOME FLIERS

CAN YOU PUT THESE AERIAL ANIMALS IN THE CORRECT PLACE ON THE SUDOKU GRID, FOLLOWING THE RULES BELOW?

SNOWY OWL    VAMPIRE BAT    MOSQUITO    HAWK

**THE RULES:**
EACH ANIMAL CAN ONLY APPEAR ONCE IN EACH ROW, COLUMN AND BOX.

ANSWERS ON PAGES 76-77    53

# MUTE SWAN
## (Cygnus olor)

**WOW!**
THE MUTE SWAN IS ONE OF THE HEAVIEST FLYING BIRDS.

**AMAZING!**
DESPITE THEIR NAME, MUTE SWANS AREN'T SILENT - THEY MAKE A RANGE OF GRUNTING AND HISSING NOISES.

**AWESOME!**
MUTE SWANS ARE BORN A GREYISH-BROWN COLOUR AND TURN WHITE WITHIN A YEAR.

**AWESOME!**
DESPITE THEIR SHORT LEGS, MUTE SWANS CAN RUN QUICKLY AND ARE ABLE TO TAKE OFF FROM LAND OR WATER.

Animal class: Bird

| | |
|---|---|
| Home: | Europe, Asia |
| Lifespan: | Over 10 years |
| Length: | 1.4m–1.6m (4½ft–5½ft) |
| Weight: | 10kg–12kg (1½st–2st) |

**Diet:**
Graceful swans dine out on water plants, insects, frogs, worms, small fish and snails.

**Hunting style:**
A swan's long neck is the perfect tool for collecting food from riverbeds. They also take in grit which they need to break down their food.

**Strong wings:**
These strong creatures have large, powerful wings with a wingspan of up to 240cm (94in). If threatened they will use their wings to attack rather than their beak.

**Deadly rating:**
Medium. Nesting swans fiercely defend their territory and can become very aggressive. A whack from their strong wings could result in injury, especially to the eyes, to anyone getting too close.

## FOOD CHAIN

Snail     Mute Swan     Fox

# EUROPEAN HERRING GULL

## *(Larus argentatus)*

RATED

**Animal class: Bird**

| | |
|---|---|
| Home: | Europe |
| Lifespan: | Up to 30 years |
| Length: | Up to 66cm (26in) |
| Weight: | 1.5kg (3$\frac{1}{3}$lb) |

Diet:

Noisy seagulls enjoy a varied diet including fish, earthworms and crustaceans. They will also scavenge what they can from human rubbish.

Hunting style:

Rubbish makes up half of a gull's food intake so they will take any opportunity to scour landfill sites and peck open bin bags.

Deadly rating:

Medium. Greedy gulls often try to steal food from humans and their sharp bills can cause injury. They are particularly dangerous because they don't fear people.

**WOW!**
THE EUROPEAN HERRING GULL HAS DECLINED IN NUMBERS BY 50% IN THE LAST 30 YEARS BUT NOBODY KNOWS WHY.

# FLYING SQUIRREL

## *(Pteromyini)*

**AMAZING!**
FLYING SQUIRRELS CAN COVER UP TO 45M (150FT) IN A SINGLE GLIDE.

**Animal class: Mammal**

| | |
|---|---|
| Home: | North America, Canada |
| Lifespan: | Average of 6 years |
| Length: | 20cm-30cm (8in-12in) |
| Weight: | Up to 140g (5oz) |

Diet:

Under the cover of darkness, flying squirrels forage for berries, nuts, fungi and birds' eggs.

Hunting style:

Flying squirrels actually glide rather than fly. A membrane that stretches from wrist to ankle acts like a parachute and they use their tails to steer and brake until they hit their target tree.

Deadly rating:

Low. Some species of flying squirrel carry the bacteria that causes typhus fever so people are advised to keep their distance from these furry creatures.

RATED

# WORD LADDER

COMPLETE THIS PUZZLE TO REVEAL THE NAME OF A DEFENSIVE BIRD WHICH, ALTHOUGH VERY RARE, HAS BEEN KNOWN TO ATTACK AND KILL PEOPLE IN THE WILD.

## THE RULES

WORK OUT WHICH LETTERS NEED TO GO IN THE BLANK BOXES BELOW – EACH LETTER WILL FORM THE END OF ONE WORD AND THE BEGINNING OF ANOTHER. THE FIRST ONE HAS BEEN DONE TO SHOW YOU HOW.

ADDING THE 'S' MAKES THE WORDS 'MISS' AND 'STAR'.

M

M I S S T A R

S N O I S H

B A N A N N T

R U I G H T

THE BIRD IS:

# BEARDED VULTURE

## (Gypaetus barbatus)

RATED

**Animal class: Bird**

| | |
|---|---|
| Home: | Europe |
| Lifespan: | Mean of 21.4 years |
| Length: | Average of 1.15m (3ft 7in) |
| Weight: | Average of 5.7kg (12½lb) |

**Diet:**
This scavenger feeds almost exclusively on animal bones.

**Hunting style:**
Bearded vultures collect bones from carcasses. They drop bigger bones from a great height to break them before devouring the bone marrow inside.

**Deadly rating:**
Low. The bearded vulture may look menacing but it causes little concern for humans – unless you happen to be walking by when those bones fall from the sky!

**AMAZING!**
THE BEARDED VULTURE CAN DIGEST SMALL BONES THAT HAVE BEEN SWALLOWED WHOLE.

# PEREGRINE FALCON

## (Falco peregrinus)

RATED

**WOW!**
PEREGRINE FALCONS HAVE AN IMPRESSIVE WINGSPAN OF UP TO 1.10M (3FT 6IN).

**RECORD BREAKER**
THE PEREGRINE FALCON IS THE FASTEST ANIMAL IN THE WORLD, CAPABLE OF REACHING SPEEDS OF AT LEAST 200 KM/H (124 MPH).

**Animal class: Bird**

| | |
|---|---|
| Home: | All continents except Antarctica |
| Lifespan: | Up to 17 years |
| Length: | 35.5cm-48cm (14in-19in) |
| Weight: | 0.5kg-1.6kg (1¾lb-3½lb) |

**Diet:**
Predatory peregrines feast on other birds, including pigeons, doves, waterfowl and grouse.

**Hunting style:**
Powerful peregrines hunt from above. After spying their prey, they swoop down to capture it mid-flight.

**Deadly rating:**
Low. With their sharp beaks and territorial instincts, if a falcon chose to attack a human serious injury could occur.

# Snowy Owl
## (Desmodontidae)

**RATED**

**AWESOME!**
SNOWY OWLS CAN SURVIVE AT TEMPERATURES AS LOW AS -40°C (-40°F).

**AMAZING!**
SNOWY OWLS ARE ACTIVE BOTH AT NIGHT AND IN THE DAYTIME.

**WOW!**
SOME SNOWY OWLS MIGRATE TO CANADA, NORTH AMERICA, EUROPE AND ASIA.

Animal class: Bird

Home: Arctic
Lifespan: Average of 10 years
Length: 50cm-71cm (20in-28in)
Weight: 1.5kg-3kg (3½lbs-6½lbs)

Diet:
The magnificent snowy owl loves lemmings, gobbling up to 1,600 of the rodents a year. They also feast on fish, rabbits and birds.

Hunting style:
Snowy owls perch patiently watching for prey before flying off to snatch their victim in their pointy claws. With sharp eyesight and a keen sense of smell, snowy owls can also track down animals that are hiding underneath snow or vegetation.

Brave defence:
Territorial snowy owls aggressively defend their nests which they build on the ground. They will fend off animals much bigger than themselves, including wolves.

Deadly rating:
Medium. If a person came too close to its nest a snowy owl could fly fast enough to knock them over. It could also cause serious damage with its razor sharp talons.

## FOOD CHAIN

 Berries   Lemming   Snowy owl

# JAPANESE GIANT HORNET

## (Vespa mandarinia japonica)

**AWESOME!**
JUST ONE GIANT JAPANESE HORNET CAN KILL 40 EUROPEAN HONEY BEES WITHIN A MINUTE.

Animal class: Invertebrate

Home: Japan
Length: 5cm (2in)

Diet:
Deadly hornets feast on a wide range of insects.

Hunting style:
These savage insects dismember their prey before returning to the hive with the most nutritious body parts.

Deadly rating:
Extremely high. The hornet's venom is strong enough to dissolve human flesh and a sting can be fatal without treatment.

# AUSTRALIAN MAGPIE

## (Cracticus tibicen)

Animal class: Bird

Home:
Australia, New Guinea
Length:
37cm-43cm ($14\frac{1}{2}$in-17in)
Weight: 220g-350g ($\frac{1}{2}$lb-$\frac{3}{4}$lb)
Diet:
Australian magpies enjoy a varied diet including walnuts, figs, earthworms, snails, spiders, ants, frogs and mice.

Hunting style:
Magpies are ground feeders. They pace open areas searching for food and use their bills to probe the earth or overturn debris.

**WOW!**
AUSTRALIAN MAGPIES ARE A PROTECTED SPECIES IN AUSTRALIA.

Deadly rating:
Medium. During breeding season magpies can become highly aggressive and have been known to attack pedestrians and cyclists causing head injuries.

# TSETSE FLY

## (Glossina)

**WOW!**
FOSSILS OF TSETSE FLIES THAT LIVED 34 MILLION YEARS AGO HAVE BEEN FOUND.

Animal class: Invertebrate

Home: Africa
Length: 6mm-16mm ($\frac{1}{4}$in-$\frac{3}{4}$in)

Diet:
The tiny tsetse fly feeds on the blood of humans, domestic animals and wild game.

Hunting style:
Tsetse flies use their serrated mouth to saw through skin and suck out their victim's blood.

Deadly rating:
High. These bloodsuckers can carry the parasite which causes sleeping sickness, a disease that is usually fatal if left untreated.

# BARRED OWL

## (Strix varia)

Animal class: Bird

Home: USA, Canada
Length: 53cm (21in)
Weight: Up to 720g ($1\frac{1}{2}$lb)
Diet:
Birds, fish, reptiles, small mammals, amphibians and invertebrates are all on the menu for these woodland owls.

**AWESOME!**
BARRED OWLS WILL DIVE INTO WATER TO CATCH FISH.

Hunting style:
The barred owl prefers to hunt from a perch, spotting prey from above before diving down to snare it.

Deadly rating:
Low. Attacks on hikers have been reported but most owls don't pose a risk to humans.

# ODD GULL OUT

CAN YOU PUT THESE HERRING GULLS INTO PAIRS TO DISCOVER WHICH ONE DOESN'T HAVE A MATCH?

A

B

C

D

E

F

G

# FACT FINDER

CROSS OUT THE FOLLOWING FROM THE GRID BELOW TO REVEAL A GRUESOME FACT ABOUT THE SNOWY OWL.

CLOTHES

LANGUAGES

COLOURS

SHAPES

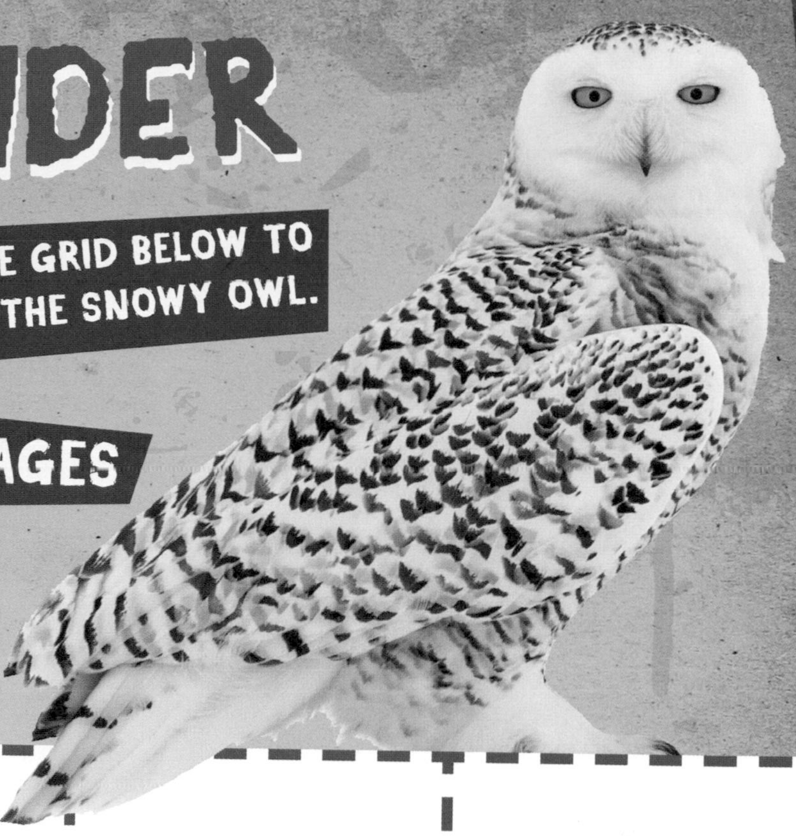

| | | | |
|---|---|---|---|
| CIRCLE | IT | SWALLOWS | RED |
| FRENCH | PREY | GREEN | JAPANESE |
| WHOLE | TROUSERS | TRIANGLE | THEN |
| SOCKS | BLUE | REGURGITATES | SQUARE |
| T-SHIRT | THE | SPANISH | BONES |

THE SNOWY OWL FACT IS:

ANSWERS ON PAGES 76–77

# INTRODUCING THE PLANT EATERS...

**AMAZING!**
GORILLAS SHARE 98.3% OF THEIR GENETIC CODE WITH HUMANS.

# GORILLA
*(Gorilla gorilla)*

**WOW!**
GORILLAS HAVE SMELLY ARMPITS AFTER STRENUOUS EXERCISE!

Animal class: Mammal

| | |
|---|---|
| Home: | Africa |
| Lifespan: | 35-40 years |
| Height: | Up to 1.8m (6ft) |
| Weight: | Up to 175kg (27½st) |

**Diet:**
Ginormous gorillas prefer a vegetarian diet of fruit, leaves, plant stems, roots and flowers, although they will also munch on ants and termites. They need a lot of food and an adult male may consume more that 18kg (40lb) of vegetation in a day.

**Hunting style:**
Gorillas are foragers using their amazing strength to break and tear vegetation. They are fussy about what they eat and use their dexterous hands to pick out the parts they want to consume.

**Brave defence:**
Mighty gorillas live in close-knit family groups led by a dominant male. He will defend his family by roaring loudly and beating his chest to warn off intruders. If that doesn't work, he will charge.

**Deadly rating:**
Medium. A gorilla needs to be provoked before it will attack a human but with their immense size and bulk, a confrontation could cause serious injury to a person and even prove fatal.

**AWESOME!**
THE GORILLA IS THE WORLD'S LARGEST PRIMATE.

## FOOD CHAIN

Vegetation

Termite

Gorilla

# CASSOWARY

## (Casuarius)

**AWESOME!**

CASSOWARIES HAVE FEARSOME, DAGGER LIKE CLAWS WHICH ARE UP TO 12CM (4¾IN) LONG.

Animal class: Bird

| | |
|---|---|
| Home: | Australia, New Guinea |
| Length: | Up to 2m (6½ft) |
| Weight: | Up to 47kg (7½st) |

Diet: Healthy cassowaries feast mainly on fruit but they also enjoy flowers, fungi, mice, frogs and fish.
Hunting style: Tough cassowaries collect fruit that has fallen from trees. Each bird defends its own tree from others and moves on once all the fruit has gone.
Deadly rating: High. A cornered or wounded cassowary can be highly dangerous. It will leap into the air and kick with such force it could damage vital organs or cause internal bleeding.

# GELADA BABOON

## (Theropithecus gelada)

**WOW!**

GELADAS FORM FAMILY UNITS WITH A MALE LEADER.

Animal class: Mammal

| | |
|---|---|
| Home: | Ethiopia |
| Length: | 50cm-74cm (19³⁄₄in-29in) |
| Weight: | 13kg-21kg (2st-3¼st) |

Diet: Grass is top of the menu for vegetarian geladas who spend up to 10 hours a day munching green shoots and seeds.
Hunting style: When it comes to feeding, geladas have a laid back style. They spend most of their day sitting on their padded bottoms grazing on grass.
Deadly rating: Low. Geladas are mainly peaceful creatures but they have been known to violently attack humans - you wouldn't want to be on the receiving end of those sharp claws!

# WILD BOAR

## (Sus scrofa)

**WOW!**

AN ADULT MALE CAPE BUFFALO IS CAPABLE OF KILLING A LION IN DEFENCE.

**WOW!**

MALE BOARS' TUSKS NEVER STOP GROWING.

Animal class: Mammal

| | |
|---|---|
| Home: | Europe, Asia, North Africa |
| Length: | 55cm-120cm (21³⁄₄in-47¹⁄₂in) |
| Weight: | Up to 100kg (15³⁄₄st) |

Diet: Wild boars dine on a huge variety of food including roots, nuts, berries, leaves, snakes, frogs, fish and bird eggs.
Hunting style: Bulky boars use their acute sense of smell to track down prey.
Deadly rating: High. Wild boars can be extremely dangerous. Males have sharp tusks which are capable of ripping flesh open.

# CAPE BUFFALO

## (Syncerus caffer)

Animal class: Mammal

| | |
|---|---|
| Home: | Africa |
| Length: | 1.7m-3.4m (5¹⁄₂ft-11ft) |
| Weight: | Up to 590kg (93st) |

Diet: Cape buffalo eat grass, grass and more grass.
Hunting style: These big beasts graze at night or in the cooler parts of the day.
Deadly rating: High. Cape buffalo are a dangerous combination of short-tempered and powerful. They gore or kill over 200 people a year.

# ELEPHANT OBSERVATION

LOOK CLOSELY AT THESE PICTURES OF A FAMILY OF ELEPHANTS ON THE MOVE. CAN YOU SPOT TEN DIFFERENCES BETWEEN THEM?

TICK A BOX AS YOU SPOT EACH DIFFERENCE.

1. ☐   3. ☐   5. ☐   7. ☐   9. ☐
2. ☐   4. ☐   6. ☐   8. ☐   10. ☐

# ANIMAL MIX-UP

UNSCRAMBLE THESE ANIMAL ANAGRAMS TO REVEAL THE NAMES OF SOME OF THE WORLD'S DEADLIEST PLANT LOVERS.

1. G I O L R R L A

☐ ☐ ☐ ☐ ☐ ☐ ☐ ☐

2. S T O I R C H

☐ ☐ ☐ ☐ ☐ ☐ ☐

3. P P O I H O P T M A S U

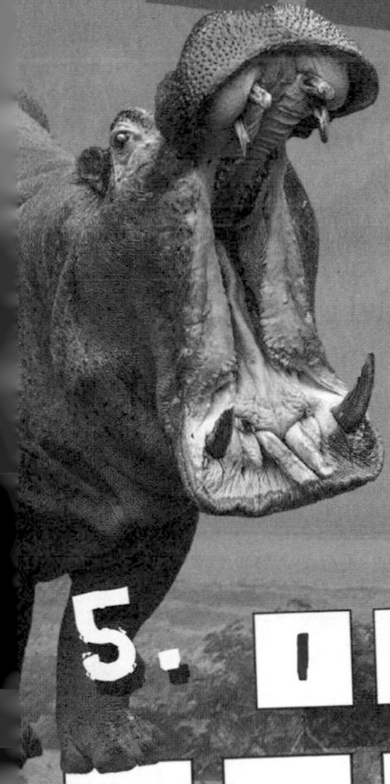

☐ ☐ ☐ ☐ ☐ ☐ ☐ ☐ ☐ ☐ ☐ ☐ ☐

4. T E E H A N P L

☐ ☐ ☐ ☐ ☐ ☐ ☐ ☐

5. I N C O R E R H O S

☐ ☐ ☐ ☐ ☐ ☐ ☐ ☐ ☐ ☐

6. D I L W  R B O A

☐ ☐ ☐ ☐  ☐ ☐ ☐

# AFRICAN ELEPHANT
## (Loxodonta africana)

RATED

**AMAZING!**
AN ELEPHANT'S TRUNK CONTAINS ABOUT 100,000 DIFFERENT MUSCLES.

**WOW!**
AN ELEPHANT'S ENORMOUS EARS RADIATE HEAT TO HELP KEEP IT COOL.

Animal class: Mammal

| | |
|---|---|
| Home: | Africa |
| Lifespan: | Up to 70 years |
| Height: | 3m-3.7m (9ft 10in-12ft) |
| Weight: | 4,000kg-7,000kg (630st-1102st) |

Diet:
Hungry elephants can consume up to 150kg (330lb) of food a day.
They feast on roots, tree bark, grasses and fruit.

Hunting style:
These mighty beasts wander for vast distances foraging for food. They use their tusks to dig for food and to strip bark from trees. Their long trunks come in handy for picking fruit.

Deadly tusks:
An African elephant's long, sharp tusks are just one of its defence mechanisms.
These magnificent teeth never stop growing and can be as long as 3m (10ft).

**WOW!**
THE AFRICAN ELEPHANT IS THE LARGEST LAND MAMMAL IN THE WORLD.

Deadly rating:
Medium. Despite their huge size, elephants are generally peaceful animals and will only attack if threatened. An attack might include being charged at, gored by its tusks, trampled on and hit with its trunk.

## FOOD CHAIN

Vegetation

Elephant

# BLUE WILDEBEEST

*(Connochaetes taurinus)*

**WOW!**
THE BIG BISON IS NORTH AMERICA'S HEAVIEST LAND ANIMAL.

**WOW!**
WILDEBEEST CALVES LEARN TO WALK AT A FEW MINUTES OLD AND CAN KEEP UP WITH THE HERD WITHIN DAYS.

Animal class: Mammal

Home: Africa
Length: Up to 2.4m (8ft)
Weight: Up to 290kg (45½st)
Diet: Vegetarian wildebeests enjoy nibbling grasses, shoots and leaves.

Hunting style: Active wildebeests graze constantly throughout the day and night.

Deadly rating: Medium. Wildebeests travel in large herds and stampede at speeds of up to 80 km/h (50 mph) when under threat – getting in their way could prove fatal.

# AMERICAN BISON

*(Bison bison)*

Animal class: Mammal

Home: North America
Length: 2.1m-3.5m (7ft-11½ft)
Weight: 422kg-998kg (66½st-157st)
Diet: Bisons keep their bulky frame by feasting on grasses, herbs, shrubs and twigs.

Hunting style: Bisons are grazers who regurgitate their food to chew as cud before it's digested.

Deadly rating: Medium. Bisons have sharp, curved horns and can easily outrun humans. They will attack if provoked.

# WHITE LIPPED PECCARY

*(Tayassu pecari)*

**WOW!**
PECCARIES HAVE A STRONG ODOUR AND CAN OFTEN BE SMELT BEFORE THEY ARE SEEN.

Animal class: Mammal

Home: Central and South America
Length: 90cm-139cm (3ft-4½ft)
Weight: Up to 22kg (3½st)
Diet: These hog-like animals eat mostly fruit but will consume leaves, stems, nuts and animal parts when fruit is scarce.

Hunting style: Determined peccaries will travel great distances to find their food.

Deadly rating: Medium. White lipped peccaries are the most dangerous species of peccary. They will use their sharp tusks to defend themselves if feeling threatened.

# GREEN IGUANA

*(Iguana iguana)*

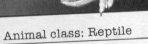

Animal class: Reptile

Home: Central America, The Caribbean, Brazil, Mexico
Length: Up to 2m (6½ft)
Weight: Up to 5kg (11lb)
Diet: Leaves, flowers and fruit are top of the list for hungry iguanas.

**WOW!**
TOUGH IGUANAS CAN JUMP FROM TREES AS HIGH AS 12M (40FT) TO THE GROUND WITHOUT HARMING THEMSELVES.

Hunting style: These laid-back reptiles spend most of their day basking in the sun, wandering off occasionally to grab a bite to eat.

Deadly rating: Medium. Iguanas have strong jaws and sharp teeth and although bites to humans are rare, if they do happen, they can cause serious injuries.

# HIPPOPOTAMUS
### (Hippopotamus amphibius)

RATED

**WOW!**
HIPPOS CAN HOLD THEIR BREATH UNDERWATER FOR AS LONG AS FIVE MINUTES.

Animal class: Mammal

| | |
|---|---|
| Home: | Africa |
| Lifespan: | Up to 40 years |
| Length: | Average of 2.8m-4m (9ft-13ft) |
| Weight: | 1,300kg-2,500kg (205st-394st) |

**WOW!**
HIPPOS YAWN AS A THREAT.

**Diet:**
Hungry hippos eat grass and a lot of it. They can consume up to 36kg (80lbs) during one long graze.

**Hunting style:**
Hippos spend their days submerged in water, coming out at night to feed. As the sun sets they travel to look for grass, sometimes walking up to 9½km (6 miles) a night.

**Killer jaws:**
Hefty hippos have incredibly powerful jaws which are strong enough to snap a canoe in half with just one bite. The sharp teeth which fill their jaws can grow as long as 50cm (1ft 8in).

**Deadly rating:**
High. Hippos are considered dangerous animals as they can be unpredictable and aggressive. They have been known to charge at small boats, capsizing them and throwing passengers into the water. Passengers then risk being killed by the hippo or drowning.

**AWESOME!**
THE COMMON HIPPOPOTAMUS IS ONE OF THE WORLD'S HEAVIEST LAND ANIMALS.

**FOOD CHAIN**

Vegetation

Hippopotamus

# TRICKY TEASER

A  B  C  D  E  F  G  H

| 1 | 2 | 3 | 4 | 5 | 6 | 7 | 8 |
|---|---|---|---|---|---|---|---|
|   |   |   |   |   |   |   |   |

CAN YOU REARRANGE THE STRIPS TO PUT THIS IGUANA IMAGE BACK IN THE RIGHT ORDER? WRITE THE CORRECT LETTER ORDER IN THE BOXES.

ANSWERS ON PAGES 76-77

71

# RHINOCEROS

*(Rhinocerotoidea)*

RATED

**WOW!**
RHINOS HAVE EXTREMELY THICK SKIN OF ABOUT 2.5CM (1IN) ON THEIR BACK AND FLANKS WHICH ACTS AS ARMOUR AGAINST THE HORNS OF OTHER RHINOS.

Animal class: Mammal

| | |
|---|---|
| Home: | Africa and Asia |
| Lifespan: | Up to 35 years |
| Length: | Up to 4.2m (13½ft) |
| Weight: | 1,600kg-4,000kg (252st-630st) |

Diet:
Black rhinos feast on fruit and leaves while white rhinos graze on grasses.

Hunting style:
Bulky black rhinos use their lips to pick their food from trees. White rhinos wander with their heads to the ground, munching as they go.

Deadly rating:
High. Rhinos will charge at anything they see as a threat. With their deadly horns and massive bulk, you wouldn't want a close encounter with these creatures!

# OSTRICH

*(Struthio camelus)*

RATED

Animal class: Bird

| | |
|---|---|
| Home: | Africa |
| Lifespan: | 40-45 years |
| Height: | Average of 2m (6½ft) |
| Weight: | 100kg-159kg (15¾st-25st) |

Diet:
Towering ostriches mainly feast on plants, roots and seeds but will also eat small creatures such as insects or lizards.

Hunting style:
An ostrich's long neck is perfectly designed to easily reach plant vegetation.

Deadly rating:
Extremely high. Ostriches have long, sharp claws and powerful legs – their aggressive kicks could seriously injure or kill a human.

**AMAZING!**
THE OSTRICH IS THE LARGEST BIRD IN THE WORLD BUT IT CAN'T FLY.

# SEQUENCE SPOT

**LOOK CAREFULLY AT THE HIGHLIGHTED SEQUENCE BELOW – CAN YOU SPOT IT THREE MORE TIMES IN THE GRID?**

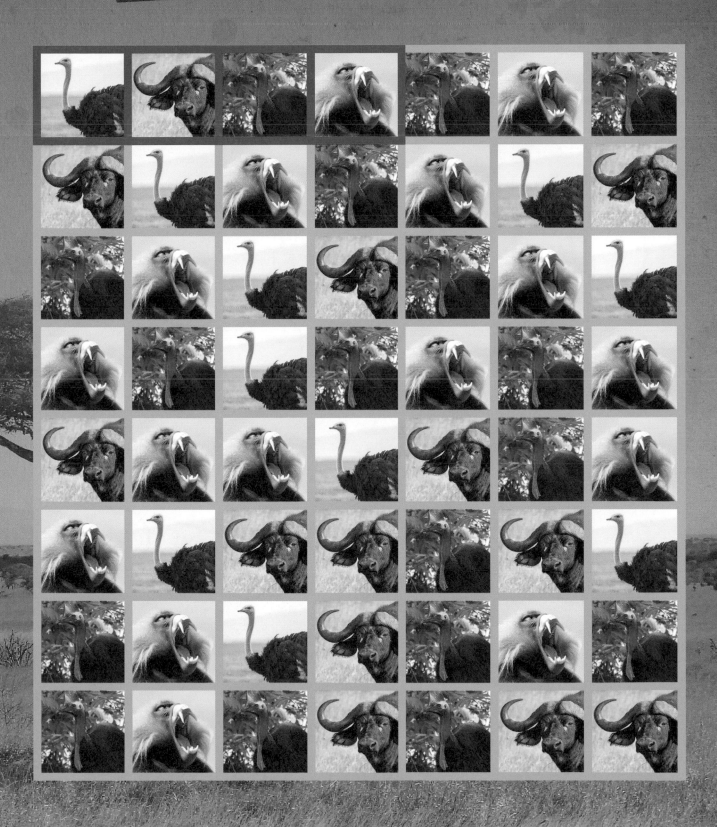

# QUIZ TIME

TEST YOUR NEWFOUND KNOWLEDGE OF PLANT LOVING ANIMALS WITH THI FUN QUIZ. TICK TRUE OR FALSE TO ANSWER EACH QUESTION.

1. THE GORILLA IS THE WORLD' LARGEST PRIMATE.

TRUE    FALSE

2. WILD BOARS ARE FUSSY EATERS

TRUE

FALSE

3. AN ELEPHANT'S EARS HELP KEEP IT COOL.

TRUE

FALSE

4. GREEN IGUANAS LOVE BASKING IN THE SUN.

TRUE    FALSE

5. WILDEBEESTS ARE SLOW MOVING ANIMALS

TRUE    FALSE

**6. HIPPOS SPEND MOST OF THE DAY IN WATER.**

TRUE  FALSE

**7.GELADA BABOONS LIVE ALONE.**

TRUE

FALSE

**8. RHINOS HAVE THICK SKIN.**

TRUE

FALSE

**9.AMERICAN BISON LIVE IN AFRICA.**

TRUE

FALSE

**10. OSTRICHES CAN'T FLY.**

TRUE  FALSE

ANSWERS ON PAGES 76-77 75

# ANSWERS

## PAGE 11
### PREDATOR PUZZLE

## PAGE 12
### WHICH ONE?
Great white shark.

## PAGE 13
### ICY MAZE

## PAGE 16
### DEADLY SUMS
Black mamba = 57
Poison dart frog = 64
Deathstalker scorpion = 52
Brazilian huntsman spider = 59
Poison dart frog is the
most poisonous.

## PAGE 20
### WHICH WAY?

## PAGE 21
### WORD PLAY
Some words you can make are:
DEAD, LIST, EAT, ATE, LEAD, IS,
ADD, LIE, DEAL, STEAL.

## PAGE 25
### SHARK SIZES
2,6,5,4,3,8,7,1.

## PAGE 26
### RECORD BREAKER
The box jellyfish is the most
venomous animal in the world.

## PAGE 27
### CREATURE COUNT
Bluefish – 10, Needlefish – 9,
Barracuda – 4.

## PAGE 30
### OCEAN PUZZLE

## PAGES 34-35
### SEA CREATURE QUIZ
1. Saltwater crocodile.
2. Red lion fish.
3. Number plate.
4. Bluefish.
5. Box jellyfish.
6. Stingray.
7. Stonefish.
8. Tiger Shark
9. Box jellyfish.

## PAGE 39
### DINO DIFFERENCES

## PAGE 40
### SHADOW MATCH
a – Diplodocus, b – Tyrannosaurus,
c – Triceratops, d – Stegosaurus.

## PAGE 41
### T-REX TEASER
It could crunch through bone.

## PAGE 44
### NEXT IN LINE
1 - Spinosaurus.
2 - Diplodocus.
3 - Stegosaurus.
4 - Coelophysis.

## PAGE 48
### UP CLOSE
1 – E.
2 – C.
3 – A.
4 – D.
5 – B.